Conflict Simulation Group

Occasional Papers no 1

Sussex Sorrows

Bibliografische Information der Deutschen Nationalbibliothek:
Die Deutsche Nationalbibliothek verzeichnet diese Publikation in der Deutschen
Nationalbibliografie; detaillierte bibliografische Daten sind im Internet über
http://dnb.dnb.de abrufbar.
© 2022 J. Wintjes/S. Pielström
Herstellung und Verlag: BoD – Books on Demand, Norderstedt
ISBN: 978-3-7568-5235-2

dedicated to the memory of

Major General Frederick Bartleby Bondsborough KCBE (1829–1913)

"They don't make them like him anymore."

PREFACE

The Prussian *Kriegsspiel* is a strange beast. While few would call the Prussian army under-researched, an important element of the Prussian army reforms in the 19th c. and something that set the Prussian army apart from all other armies in Europe for nearly half a century has seen to date very little scholarly attention. One reason may well be that researching the Prussian *Kriegsspiel* requires gaining proficiency in running it, as properly understanding the character of the published rulesets is otherwise next to impossible.

When running *Kriegsspiele*, one will invariably be struck by how powerful the *Kriegsspiel* is in exposing participants to friction and fog-of-war; indeed, the authors would venture so far as to claim that no other wargame, historical or modern, comes even close in that regard. Running *Kriegsspiel*-type wargames is therefore an experience worth the while even beyond purely academic interest, as the authors' experience has shown.

We publish these present rules with the hope that they might inspire others to try running a *Kriegsspiel* – and with a caveat: Participation in a *Kriegsspiel* can be a rewarding experience, but fun may not be the first thing participants associate with it; as a staff officer from a NATO country once told the authors: "I really learned a lot, but the fog-of-war was the most unsettling experience of my career."

This booklet is dedicated to our families who have the quite questionable honour of living – and sometimes making up – with wargamers.

CONTENT

1. Introduction.

In the mid-1870s, Prussian army captain Jakob Meckel published a series of notes on the use of the Prussian *Kriegsspiel*, eventually culminating in a new set of rules; his work proved to be eminently influential, and Meckel, who would eventually rise to the rank of general, entered the annals of *Kriegsspiel* history as the *Kriegspiel*'s most important theoretician. This is not the place to recount the developmental history of the world's first true conflict simulation in any detail;[1] it is sufficient to say that Meckel's crucial contribution to the development of the *Kriegsspiel* lay in expanding it beyond its original character as a tactical battlefield simulation, adding operational and "strategic" (for which "theatre" is probably the best modern equivalent) levels to it.

About a hundred years later Trevor Nevitt Dupuy first published a new methodology for conflict simulations, the so-called quantified judgement model (QJM), which had a significant impact on the study of conflicts for purposes of analysis and prediction.[2] At the heart of the QJM lay the concept of calculating losses by employing a formula which accounted for a variety of aspects influencing the outcome of a battle by including different factors to the equation, usually between 0 and 2. In doing so, Dupuy to some extent followed – unknowingly – the basic conflict resolution mechanism at the core of the Prussian *Kriegsspiel*; the main difference between the QJM and the Prussian *Kriegsspiel* is that the former is about attrition, while the latter is about probabilities; the QJM calculates the percentage of forces lost in combat, while the *Kriegsspiel* calculates the probability of a specific

---

[1] For a brief overview see J. Wintjes. 2022. A School for War – A Brief History of the Prussian Kriegsspiel, in: C. Turnitsa/C. Blais/A. Tolk (eds.). *Simulation and Wargaming*. Hoboken:Wiley, 25-64.
[2] T. N. Dupuy. 1979. *Numbers, Predictions and War*. Indianapolis: Bobbs-Merrill.

outcome; furthermore, while in the QJM factors are highly variable depending on the various circumstances influencing the outcome of a battle, in the *Kriegsspiel* only 1.33 or 1.5 and multiples thereof are used to calculate the probability of success or failure; once the outcome of an engagement has been determined, there are fixed loss ratios.

The simulation presented in this small book is essentially a combination of the two approaches; it uses Meckel's approach to operational wargaming, tries to heed his call for keeping things as simple as possible, and while at its heart there is a classic Prussian die table for determining the outcome of an engagement by using a D6, modifiers similar to the factors used by the QJM are employed to modify troop strength before using the die table; the process is described in more detail below. The scenarios for which the authors designed the present set of rules are all based on late 19th c. invasion novel literature and focus on a French invasion force landing in Sussex in the early 1880s, hence the somewhat outlandish titles of the main set of rules and the urban warfare expansion. However, the basic mechanics could be used to depict any conflict of the industrial age from the Crimean War down to the Balkan Wars of the early 1910s, and with some adaptation even beyond that.

The authors have used "Sussex Sorrows" and its companion, "Doom of Eastbourne", a tactical version focusing on urban warfare, successfully for several years both with early-career military decision makers and with participants of staff-college courses. It can be run both in person and online, and it has proven to be quite successful in simulating all those issues arising from fog-of-war. Just like the Meckel *Kriegsspiel*, "Sussex Sorrows" is a simulation that is run exclusively by facilitators, which for participants offers the key advantage of being more accessible than any normal rules-based simulation. Participants do not have to engage with the rules at all and can fully concentrate on the scenario; this is particularly advantageous in educational contexts where time is limited and training participants in how to run the simulation reduces the time available for actually running it. Of course, the facilitators running "Sussex Sorrows" need to have a good command of the rules, and particularly for larger scenarios it is advisable to a sizeable number of facilitators available.

"Sussex Sorrows" could be run in turns, but the authors have made the experience that participants gain the most from it when they experience it as a real-time simulation. This does add, however, significantly to the facilitators' workload. In a larger operational scenario where several divisional teams are operating on both sides it is advisable to have at least one facilitator permanently assigned to each team; the authors usually run scenarios with 20 participants on each side with a team of ten facilitators.

The present booklet provides the core rules, the "Doom of Eastbourne" expansion and some special rules covering the inclusion of role-playing elements; further information can be found on the Conflict Simulation Group's website.[3] Little else is needed for running a *Kriegsspiel* based on the "Sussex Sorrows" rules; some notes on the logistics required have been provided following the rules.

---

[3] https://cosimg.github.io/

2.   General Rules.

"Sussex Sorrows" is a military simulation modelled closely after Jakob Meckel's *Kriegsspiel* of the mid-1870s. It is a facilitator-driven operational wargame aimed at training participants in processing information, communicating and making decisions under conditions of fog-of-war. Opposing teams have to work in separate rooms, create a situational picture according to the messages they receive from their units and control their forces through written orders. Communication by subordinate units is simulated by a team of facilitators that takes care of unit tracking and conflict resolution. Only the situation on the facilitators' map is considered to represent the "reality" of the simulation, whereas the teams always have to operate with an unreliable situational picture depending on their information processing skills. In line with the Prussian original, "Sussex Sorrows" provides a rather simple set of rules requiring a minimum of facilitator training. It is tailored to provide a smooth real time experience in division- to corps level operational settings, often at the expense of contemporary tactical detail. Some alterations have been made to historical game mechanics for improved scalability and ease of use, but the basic probabilities of success and defeat have been largely preserved. The scenario underlying "Sussex Sorrows", a French invasion of Britain in the early 1880s, featured regularly in British army war games of the period.

2.1.   Basic Elements.

The simulation is run on a period topographic map. Opposing forces are depicted on this map by symbols. Both traditional and digital maps can be used: on a traditional map, units will be represented by tokens, while when working with a digital version, unit symbols can be moved on the map using an editor for presentation spreadsheets or vector graphics.

The basic building blocks for the simulation are battalions of infantry, squadrons of cavalry and batteries of artillery. Smaller units should be depicted only under special circumstances; for example, if a single rifle company is left behind to guard a communications asset. Quite often it is advisable to use symbols representing larger formations as well, as for example infantry brigades still regularly moved and attacked *en bloc* during the period.

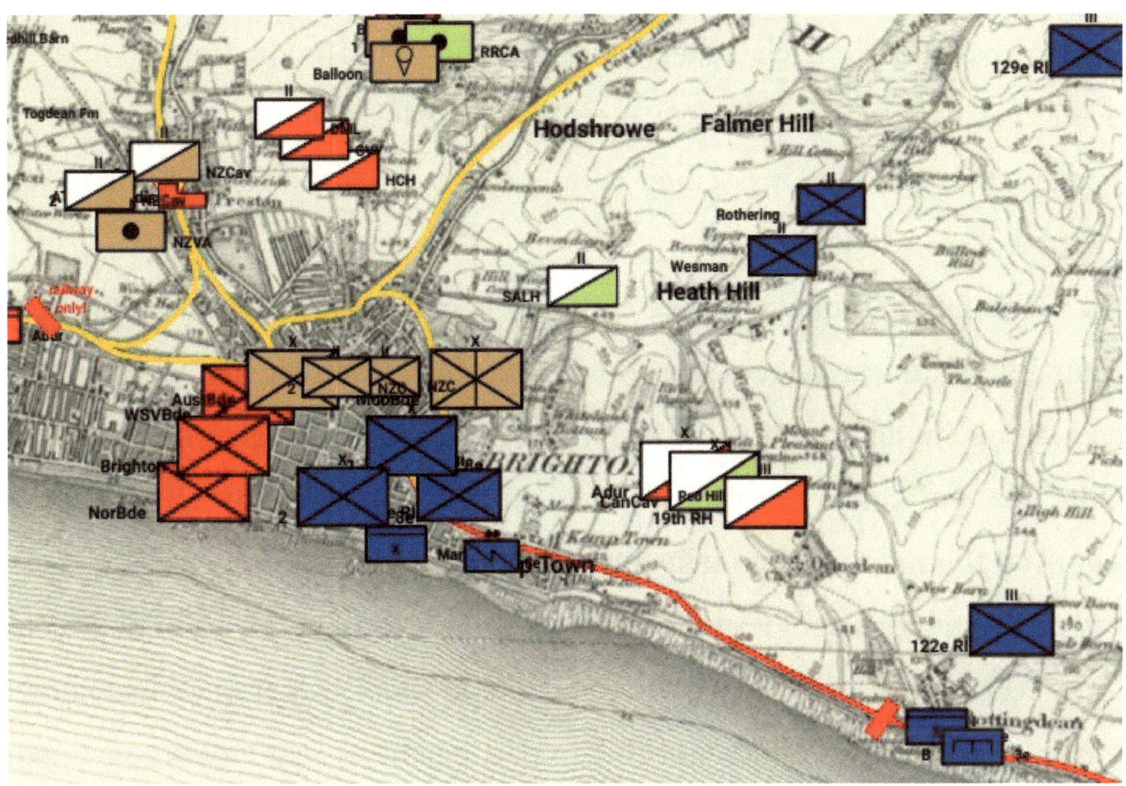

Heavy fighting around Brighton – a typical "Sussex Sorrows" map

2.3.   Messages and Orders.

Participants receive information through messages written by the facilitators; this simulates the actions of subordinate units and officers. It is left to the facilitators' discretion what units, unit commanders or patrols can see and know from their respective positions on the map. Participants can influence events by writing orders to their units and sending them to the facilitators; these orders mirror the written dispatches used on a 19th century battlefield. Each order must clearly indicate the sender and his location as well as the addressee and the latter's location as presumed by the sender; otherwise, the messenger cannot know where to carry the message and to whom to hand it over.

The facilitators will decide over any communication delays which can occur for a number of reasons: the distance a messenger has to cover is a key factor in determining how long a message will take to reach the addressee, but communication delays can also be caused by enemy action requiring the messenger to take a longer route, or when the addressee is no longer at the location determined in the message. Communication delays are a key feature of "Sussex Sorrows", and the authors' experience has shown that it is imperative to highlight this to participants – many of whom, again according to the authors' experience, will nevertheless be shocked by the effect delayed communication can have on their situational awareness.

2.4.   Subordinate Commanders.

If due to applied mission-type tactics or communication delay a situation requires a local decision, facilitators will act according to standing orders, general rules of engagement and the local commander's character and ability. For each of the subordinate commanders a brief characterization is given; see also the special rules section below.

3. Movement.

3.1. General Movement.

Units move according to the marching table below, which is derived from official British army wargaming rules from the 1890s. Heavy terrain (woodlands etc.) restrict movement by a third, built-up areas by two thirds.

infantry	**800 m**	per 10 minutes
cavalry	**1,500 m**	per 10 minutes
artillery	**1,500 m**	per 10 minutes
heavy artillery	**800 m**	per 10 minutes
messengers (horse)	**4,000 m**	per 10 minutes
messengers (foot)	**800 m**	per 10 minutes

3.2. Artillery and Vehicles.

Artillery and other assets moving in horse-drawn vehicles can cross a river or stream only by using a bridge. Field artillery on the move cannot fire instantly, it requires 3-5 minutes to unlimber and get ready to fire (horse artillery requires only 90-120 seconds). Heavy artillery, due to the need for building emplacements for the guns, will never engage the enemy within a few minutes after reaching a position. Depending on the terrain and the number of engineers employed this usually takes between 1 and 3 hours.

3.3. Reconnaissance.

Cavalry units regularly send patrols to scout the surrounding territory when on the move. They have a reconnaissance range of about 2 km, depending on the topography. When ordered to scout or monitor a certain area, the cavalry commander can also send long range patrols while remaining stationary with the bulk of his force. Unmounted units can send out foot patrols or forward picket lines to gather information. However, these move at a considerably slower pace. Moreover, foot patrols are very vulnerable to enemy cavalry in open areas. Infantry and artillery forces on the march therefore do not send out scouting parties if not explicitly ordered to do so.

3.4.   Delaying Enemy Movement.

The opponent's ability to move freely can be reduced considerably by posing a constant threat to the marching soldiers, thus forcing them to prioritize threat avoidance and adopting defensive formations over rapid movement. To do so does however require a high level of mobility and training. In open terrain, this task is performed by horse artillery, through constantly unlimbering, maybe even firing a few shots, but moving away instantly as soon as the enemy force starts adopting counter measures. Cavalry alone cannot perform delaying tactics, but should always accompany horse artillery, as the regular countermeasure against being delayed by enemy horse artillery is sending cavalry to catch it. On broken ground infantry can be deployed in skirmishing order to delay enemy movement. Other unit types cannot be relied upon to execute delaying tactics successfully. On average, a delayed force can move at half of its regular pace.

3.5.   Force and Space.

Concentration of forces is a key concept in 19th century warfare. But even though close formations are still common in the period, there are spatial limitations to concentration. Most importantly there is a limit as to the number of men that can fight at the same time along a certain length of front line. If too many troops are tasked to fight in limited space, local commanders will independently assign surplus soldiers to a reserve force that is not counted for the resolution of the current combat event.

The following figures serve as a rough guideline for estimating the space required by full-strength formations in the field:

infantry battalion (800-1000 men) in line formation:	**400 m**
infantry battalion skirmishing on broken ground:	**800 m**
infantry brigade, line formation (line of 3 bn, 3 bn in reserve):	**1,200 m**
infantry brigade, assault form. (3 bn in cols., 3 bn in reserve):	**500 m**
cavalry brigade in assault formation (8 sqn in two lines):	**300 m**
battery at regular intervals (4 field guns):	**50 m**
battery in close order (4 field guns):	**20 m**

Troops manoeuvring and moving in formation also require a certain amount of space. Insufficient manoeuvring space will result either in unit cohesion suffering or in traffic jams. The consequence of both is a reduction of the speed of movement at the facilitators' discretion.

If forces have to move through a narrow choking point – eg a bridge or a ford - the following numbers give a rough estimate of the time required to pass:

infantry battalion	**10 min**
cavalry squadron	**5 min**
gun battery	**10 min**

4. Combat

4.1. General Mechanism

As in the Prussian *Kriegsspiel*, combat is resolved by a single roll of the die, the result of which is indicated by the die table (see below). The basic chances of success correspond to the numerical proportion of the opposing forces, ie if fighting an enemy double one's strength the basic odds of success are 1:2. Each piece of artillery is counted as equivalent to 100 men. Certain circumstances lead to the fighting strength of one side being modified by one or more factors, eg if a cavalry unit is attacking scattered enemy troops, its fighting value per trooper is considered twice as large.

Example: Team BLUE has a company of 100 infantrymen scattered to scout an area. Team RED is attacking this unit with 100 cavalrymen. The basic odds ratio based on numerical strength is 1:1. As the defender is scattered, the strength of team RED is modified by the factor 2, resulting in a odds ratio of 2:1 for the attacker. The final odds ratio after considering all applicable modifying factors is used to select the correct row on the die table. The outcome of the die roll then determines the column that indicates the outcome of the engagement. For example, if the attacker throws a 3, the die table indicates "attacker spent, 30%, defender shattered, 50%"; the attack has been successful, the defender has been driven off, but the attacker has also suffered significantly and cannot continue to attack immediately.

4.2.1. Unit Quality and Status.

There are three basic unit qualities: "volunteer", "regular" and "experienced". Volunteer units are assumed to have only three quarters (quality factor 0.75) of the regular fighting strength, while experienced units have a quality factor of 1.25. Furthermore, a unit can be "fresh" (no modifiers, quality factor 1.0), "spent" (quality factor 0.75) or even "shattered" (quality factor 0.5). Both spent and shattered units are not capable of performing offensive action or forced marches. Spent units can recover and regain fresh status within 1 hour, shattered units within 2.5 hours.

Several other factors can influence the outcome of an engagement; below is a list of the most common factors which, multiplied with a unit's numerical strength to determine the final odds ratio for combat resolution. If multiple factors apply, all are regarded. The facilitators are free to modify these factors – or even include new ones – should circumstances arise during the simulation that render the listed factors inappropriate or insufficient. One should remember that calculations are unnecessary for factors that equally apply to both sides.

regular	**1**
volunteer (attacker/defender)	**0.75**
experienced (attacker/defender)	**1.25**
elite (attacker/defender)	**1.5**
spent (attacker/defender)	**0.75**
shattered (attacker/defender)	**0.5**
elevated position (attacker/defender)	**1.25**
defender dug-in	**1.5** (defender)
defender in built-up area	**1.5** (defender)
surprise attack on marching enemy	**2.0** (attacker)
assault from flank/rear	**2.0** (attacker)
cavalry vs prepared infantry or artillery	**0.5** (attacker)
infantry attacking an enemy out of formation	**1.5** (attacker)
cavalry attacking a scattered enemy	**2.0** (attacker)

The use of the factor outlined above is illustrated by the example below. Note that if a defender is shattered, the defending force is routed. It will leave behind any artillery and heavy equipment it had at its disposal.

Example: *Team RED is defending a prepared line of field fortifications with two battalions of 2,000 infantrymen in total. Team BLUE is attacking this position in a frontal assault with 3,000 infantrymen. The basic odds ratio based on numerical strength is 3:2 for the attacker. As the defender is fighting from prepared fortifications, the strength of team RED is modified by the factor 1.5; as a result, the 2,000 red defenders are counted as 2,000 x 1.5 = 3000 defenders. The final odds ratio for the die roll therefore is 1:1. The die rolls a 5. According to the die table, the defender wins the fight. The RED force is still fresh and battle-ready, it suffers 10% casualties. The attacker is routed: the BLUE battalions are shattered, fleeing in disorder, and suffer 50% casualties.*

Now RED decides to use the opportunity to counterattack their weakened opponent. RED has 1,800 men left, BLUE 1,500 men. The numerical odds are close to 1:1. However, the BLUE force is shattered, its fighting strength is therefore modified by a factor of 0.5, resulting in 1,500 x 0.5 = 750 men. RED is attacking an enemy that is out of formation, hence the strength of the RED forces is modified by the factor 1.5, resulting in 1,800 x 1.5 = 2700 men. The final odds ratio for the counterattack therefore is 2,700:750, which equals 3.6:1. This value is closer to the 4:1 than to 3:1, therefore the facilitators decide to resolve combat according to the 4:1 row. The first roll of the die gives a 4; according to the die table, the umpire has to roll again. The second roll gives a 3. As a result, the BLUE forces are further driven back and they again lose 50% of their men; their numerical strength is now down to 750 men; it will take at least an hour to regroup these men, and some more hours to get them combat ready for offensive action again. The successful RED force is now spent and has suffered 30% casualties. The remaining 1,260 men are exhausted and not ready for more offensive action in the next hour.

4.3.   Special Forms of Combat.

There are combat situations that differ somewhat from a direct, decisive encounter between attacker and defender.

Delaying Actions: Delaying actions are handled as described in chapter 3.4 and not treated as actual combat actions. They only result in the reduction of marching speed, while casualties and ammunition consumption are considered to be minor and ignored.

Artillery Duels: Artillery duels can be processed and decided in nearly the same way as regular combat actions; shattered defenders will not leave their equipment behind and can be expected to retreat before total destruction. Hence any die roll indicating "destroyed" as a result will be reduced to "shattered" (50% casualties).

Fire Missions: Fire missions occur when artillery fires at units that have no means to fight back. Fire missions are treated like artillery duels, but all negative consequences for the attacking unit beyond the consumption of ammunition are ignored.

Fire Support: Fire support can be provided by artillery batteries for infantry assaults or defences. In that case, artillery pieces are counted to the overall numbers with a field artillery piece counting as 100 men and a piece of heavy artillery counting as 200 men. If an attacker has to cross an open area covered by artillery the facilitators can allow an additional fire mission before resolving the outcome of the engagement. Should an attack supported by artillery fail, the artillery does not suffer casualties unless it is overrun by a counterattack.

5. The die table.

Combat results are based on the attacker's odds ratio. D = defender, A = attacker. Green fields indicate a success for the attacker, yellow fields success for the defender. Casualties are indicated as percent values.

results (D6)

odds ↓	1	2	3	4	5	6
1:5	A: spent 30% D: fresh 20%	A: shattered 50% D: fresh 10%	A: shattered 50% D: spent 30%	A: shattered 50% D: fresh 10%	A: destroyed D: spent 30%	A: destroyed D: spent 30%
1:4	A: spent 30% D: fresh 20%	A: fresh 20% D: fresh 10%	A: shattered 50% D: spent 30%	re-roll	A: shattered 50% D: fresh 10%	A: destroyed D: spent 30%
1:3	A: spent 30% D: fresh 20%	A: fresh 20% D: fresh 10%	re-roll	A: shattered 50% D: fresh 10%	re-roll	A: destroyed D: spent 30%
1:2	A: spent 30% D: fresh 20%	A: fresh 20% D: fresh 10%	A: shattered 50% D: fresh 10%	A: spent 30% D: shattered 50%	A: shattered 50% D: fresh 10%	A: destroyed D: spent 30%
2:3	A: spent 30% D: fresh 20%	A: fresh 20% D: fresh 10%	re-roll	A: shattered 50% D: fresh 10%	A: fresh 10% D: shattered 50%	A: destroyed D: spent 30%
1:1	A: fresh 20% D: spent 30%	A: fresh 10% D: fresh 20%	A: shattered 50% D: spent 30%	A: fresh 10% D: shattered 50%	A: shattered 50% D: fresh 10%	A: spent 30% D: destroyed
3:2	A: fresh 20% D: spent 30%	A: fresh 10% D: fresh 20%	re-roll	A: fresh 10% D: shattered 50%	A: shattered 50% D: fresh 10%	A: spent 30% D: destroyed
2:1	A: fresh 20% D: spent 30%	A: fresh 10% D: fresh 20%	A: spent 30% D: shattered 50%	A: shattered 50% D: spent 30%	A: fresh 10% D: shattered 50%	A: spent 30% D: destroyed
3:1	A: fresh 20% D: spent 30%	A: fresh 10% D: fresh 20%	re-roll	A: fresh 10% D: shattered 50%	re-roll	A: spent 30% D: destroyed
4:1	A: fresh 20% D: spent 30%	A: fresh 10% D: fresh 20%	A: spent 30% D: shattered 50%	re-roll	A: fresh 10% D: shattered 50%	A: spent 30% D: destroyed
5:1	A: fresh 20% D: spent 30%	A: fresh 10% D: shattered 50%	A: spent 30% D: shattered 50%	A: fresh 10% D: shattered 50%	A: spent 30% D: destroyed	A: spent 30% D: destroyed

6. Optional Rules

6.1. Introduction.

Below are a number of additional simulation elements and rules aimed mainly at increasing both immersion and workload of "Sussex Sorrows" participants. While they are to a certain extent optional, they add considerable to the overall experience, and the authors have made the experience that implementing them is well worth the additional effort by the facilitators, particularly, if scenarios are designed to run for a prolonged period of time.

6.2. Ammunition Management.

For simplicity's sake it is assumed that each substantial engagement uses up 20% of any unit's ammunition. Logistics elements serve to resupply and have to be directed by the participants. Units out of ammunition cannot attack and will try to avoid combat unless explicitly ordered not to; in defence they suffer a modifier of 0.5.

6.3. Casualty Management.

Participants are required to designate casualty collection points and redirect casualties if collection points run out of capacity. A lack of care for casualties will have effects at the facilitators' discretion; in general, an impact on force morale is to be expected, and subordinate commanders may question orders more often.

6.4. POW Management.

Participants are required to designate POW collection points and redirect POWs if collection points run out of capacity. This ties down military capability, as POWs have to be guarded, something actually covered in early Prussian *Kriegsspiele.* POW interrogation may offer valuable information to the participants, if only by identifying the units they belong to.

6.5. Civil-Military Interaction.

While a tactical *Kriegsspiel* may depict a battle in an environment largely free from non-combatants, an operational *Kriegsspiel* like "Sussex Sorrows" takes place in an environment where civil-military interaction is extremely likely. This is an important aspect of "Sussex Sorrows" and largely at the facilitators' discretion. Civilians might provide useful information, tend wounded (eg increasing the capabilities of casualty collection points) or take up arms. They may also take to the streets in panic, blocking roads, or provide a general nuisance by pestering participants with questions and demands. There are no hard and fast rules for inserting civilians into scenario; it is, however, well worth putting considerable effort into, as according to the authors' experience the inclusion of civil-military interaction is one of the most powerful instruments for creating immersion in an operational *Kriegsspiel*.

7. A Final Word.

The authors have made the experience that, when facilitating an operational *Kriegsspiel* like "Sussex Sorrows", two things are of utmost importance: one, the facilitators have to keep the *Kriegsspiel* running no matter what, the real-time aspect being crucial to the overall experience. And two, the facilitators should allow the participants the widest possible latitude regarding their orders, even if that can add considerably to the facilitators' workload. If a team representing a French divisional HQ decides to pressure local English bakers into holding a croissant bake-off, facilitators have to come up with a plausible and measured response – simply having a bake-off will not cause a general rebellion in a captured city; but hanging those whose products were deemed to be unsatisfactory might.

DOOM OF EASTBOURNE

1.   General Information.

"Doom of Eastbourne" is a supplement for the "Sussex Sorrows" ruleset covering urban combat in the late 19th c. The basic building blocks are infantry companies of around 100 men and individual field guns; the game is played on a topographical map. The general mechanics of "Sussex Sorrows" apply to "Doom of Eastbourne"; there are only a few minor additions.

2.   Movement.

Infantry companies can occupy anything between three and ten average-sized houses. In principle, movement is possible both through streets and through houses, though only units that are "fresh" can move through houses. Artillery pieces can be moved through streets and manhandled into gardens; they cannot take up positions in houses unless specified otherwise by the scenario.

3.   Combat.

As "Doom of Eastbourne" concentrates on urban combat, the list of modifiers has to be expanded to include the following:

defender in large building:	**4.0**
defender in stone building:	**3.0**
defender in wooden building:	**2.0**
defender in field fortification or behind barricade:	**1.5**
assault from flank/rear:	**2.0**
infantry attacking an enemy out of formation:	**1.5**
infantry attacking a scattered enemy:	**2.0**

As usual multiple modifiers may apply. Note that attacking defended positions inside houses invariably means drawing fire. Before combat is resolved according to the "Sussex Sorrows" die table, the defender can fire a salvo at the attacker; if successful, the attacker suffers losses. Refer to the percentages given in the die table; the attacker suffers the respective percentage of the defender's troop strength in losses.

Example: 100 men attack 80 men positioned in buildings. Before combat is resolved the 80 men fire at the 100 attackers. According to the die table the attackers suffer 20% losses, which in this case means 20% of the defender's strength – 16 men. Therefore, they enter combat with 84 men against the defender's 80 men.

4.   Casualties and Unit Strength Management.

Once unit strength has fallen below a certain level, the unit is out of action; it is possible to pool men from different units into one scratch unit, but for that purpose all units in question have to move back to an HQ. The number depends on the troop quality:

volunteer	**50%**
regular	**33%**
experienced	**25%**

5.   Ammunition and Supplies.

Units lose 20% ammunition per firefight. Once they are out of ammunition, defenders can carry on defending their position, but lose any modifiers associated with their position. Units out of ammunition can still attack but will take two salvos and suffer a modifier of 0.5 when combat is resolved. Units can be resupplied by supply elements. These have a maximum supply range of 200m. If a unit is positioned beyond that supply range and runs out of ammunition, it has to move back within supply range in order to resupply.

USEFUL IDIOTS AND INSUFFERABLE GENIUSES.

1.   Introduction.

As noted above, facilitators sometimes have to make independent decisions as subordinate commanders would not have the time or inclination to check back with their superiors. In an operational *Kriegsspiel*, where facilitators can represent subordinate commanders up to brigade level, this is likely to happen fairly often. As in reality higher levels in the chain of command would have a certain idea of the character and abilities – or lack thereof! – of their subordinate commanders, it is important to include the personalities of subordinate commanders in the creation of a scenario; while these can be developed solely at the facilitator's discretion, below are some suggestions for rules governing the process. However it is done, it is important to provide participants with information which offer at least some insight into the character of their subordinates.

While adding further to the facilitators' workload, the authors' experience has shown that including these elements significantly enhances immersion for the participants, particularly if the simulation runs over more than only a few hours and participants are exposed to the whims of their subordinates for longer periods of time. While presented here together with "Sussex Sorrows" and "Doom of Eastbourne", the suggestions for character creation outlined below can be applied to any facilitator-based simulation of 19th c, conflict; they could also easily be adapted to any other conflict.

2.   Character.

The general character of a subordinate commander as a military leader can be defined by three different attributes:

Tactical Competence: Tactical competence is the ability to judge the terrain and tactical situation, and to lead his force in a way that secures optimal chances of success in combat; each subordinate commander is assigned a tactical competence value. When the umpires are in doubt about what a commander would do, a roll against the tactical competence value will help them decide whether or not the commander will make the optimal choice.

Operational Understanding: Operational understanding is the ability to judge on and act according to the general operational goals of the higher-level commanders (ie the participants); each subordinate commander is assigned an operational understanding value. When in doubt, a roll against the operational understanding value can decide if the local commander understands what the participants want him to do, and whether he can act on it.

Aggression: Aggression is the willingness to directly engage the enemy. This attribute is considered in situations where it is unclear if the commander would attack. Each subordinate commander is assigned an aggression value. Commanders with the lowest aggression value (1) will at times find excuses to not carry out attack orders if the action seems to be dangerous from their point of view.

The attributes outlined above can take values between 1 and 5. Attribute rolls are done with a D6; if the result is equal to or lower than the attribute value, the roll is a success, and the commander will behave accordingly. In situations where multiple attributes can be applied, the umpires will always use the attribute with the highest value. For instance, a commander whose aggression value is higher than his tactical competence value is not unlikely to make potentially suicidal decisions.

Attribute values are not communicated to the player teams and are known only to the umpires; this depicts the real-world situation in which military deciders have to rely mostly on reputation and observations made in training environments when judging the abilities subordinate officers might show on the battlefield. Instead, scenario materials will contain hints on particularly outstanding attributes for some commanders.

3.   Specializations.

In addition to these numerical attributes, every commander has a specialization, usually rooted in the branch of service he is most familiar with. This specialization determines much of the general tactical mindset. It is another aid for the umpiring team to decide on the commander's most likely cause of action. There are four different specializations:

Infantry: The commander understands how to attack and defend a given position with infantry. He has an understanding on how to use terrain and formations to his advantage, and how to employ artillery support. He will try to achieve his goals using both ranged and close combat.

Artillery: The artillery commander is most experienced in ranged combat. He usually concentrates on securing a superior topographical position to fight from. When attacking, he will often try to concentrate fire in order to create a weak point for an attack.

Cavalry: Cavalry commanders have a reputation of being aggressive to the point of recklessness. Their preferred solution to nearly every tactical situation is charging the enemy head-on with cold steel. However, they are also used to rely heavily on mobility. In combat they try to outmanoeuvre their opponent. Cavalry commanders are often more mindful of the need for reconnaissance and the possibilities to delay enemy movements than other officers.

Navy: Officers brought up in the navy are comparable to artillery officers when it comes to out-gunning the enemy. Moreover, they often think in terms of attacking or defending strong positions. On the other hand, they are usually less experienced in using terrain than army officers.

4. Chance Throw.

If there are no commander attributes for the umpiring team to rely on in an unclear situation, especially in situations where the outcome will have a significant impact on the overall situation, a chance roll with odds of 1:1 will be applied to decide what happens.

5. Replacing Subordinates.

It is not uncommon that participants are dissatisfied with a subordinate's decisions or performance and want to replace a subordinate commander. In this case, the new commander's specialization is determined by the unit he is drawn from. To determine his attributes, the umpires roll a D6 for each attribute, divide the result by two and round it up to generate random numbers between 1 and 3. It is advisable to inform participants in advance of the fact that replacing a subordinate commander does not automatically mean he is replaced by someone more reliable or more capable.

Finally, a few notes on resources required for running "Sussex Sorrows". As noted above, apart from tokens and a topographical map little else is required in terms of hardware. Late 19th c. topographic maps produced by the British Ordnance Survey are readily available both in libraries and on the second-hand book market. The production of tokens presents little difficulties in an age where even complex printing services are readily available; the authors have for years used the cheap expedient of printing labels and gluing them to pieces of cardboard or pre-cut MDF. Sample token sheets for "Sussex Sorrows" can be found on the Conflict Simulation Group's website;[4] tokens are not even a necessary requirement – it would be entirely possible to simply write upon the maps.

Information on the British and French armies of the late 19th c. is readily available as well. The study of Victorian and Edwardian future war fiction owes much to the work of the late Ignatius Frederick Clarke.[5] His anthologies provide the best introduction to the subject, and many texts are nowadays accessible via online repositories.

In terms of general logistics, running "Sussex Sorrows" requires little more than a number of rooms (or secluded work areas) for the different teams ensuring they do not communicate with each other. Tables and chairs are useful, but entirely optional, as maps could be hung on walls or whiteboards, and messages be written while standing, adding a possible layer of friction due to the deterioration in handwriting involved.

---

[4] https://cosimg.github.io/, see "conflict simulation in the classroom".
[5] See in particular Clarke, Ignatius Frederick. 1992. *Voices prophesying war. Future wars, 1763-1749*. Oxford: Oxford University Press, and Clarke, Ignatius Frederick. 1995. *The Tale of the Next Great War 1871-1914. Fictions of future warfare and of battles still-to-come*. Liverpool: Liverpool University Press.